CONTINUUM

POEMS
BY

ARTHUR ERBE

The Poet's
Press
PITTSBURGH, PA

This is the 240th publication of The Poet's Press
Ver 1.2

THE POET'S PRESS
2209 Murray Avenue #3
Pittsburgh, PA 15217-2338

TABLE OF CONTENTS

CONTINUUM

ENDLESS RECALL

if time were to stop right now
I could recreate many moments

the mind does not forget
yesterday's wet weather

how a friend just left
with no forwarding address

all the faces I met everyday
showing their joy and sorrow

each and every shivering bird
swaying on the telephone wire

the ant hill I stomped on
as an angry twelve-year-old

a dream about being lost
without any end to the forest

the eclipse of the moon
darkness in the galaxy

time doesn't stop and the mind
rattles on with endless recall

<11>

THE
MONTHS

JANUARY

Fifteen degrees,
        a wind factor minus four,
                slight flurries expected.

My neighbor appears with
        two Comice pears,
blemished, soft to touch:

mailed from Harry & David's
        gourmet fruit of the month.

        You can eat them with a spoon

with a lingering taste of ripeness
        and anticipation:

nothing left but seeds
            parings of skin.

If Persephone had rejected
        pomegranates for pears,
        we would sense balmy breezes,
tropical heat waves.

Here salt trucks plow
        snowy roads safe.

<15>

FEBRUARY

A country woman, surviving harsh winters,

tells me
about frozen water on hillside rocks:
                    no sign of spring until it melts.
Smooth is ice when the wind is cold —
long the time
for reflection.
Twenty-seven days of anticipation
                without any hint of change;
when the ice moon freezes,
            the landscape refuses to listen —
clocks nervous as the day unwinds.

How do I go on?

None of us knows
                why we stare at the wall,

feeling the silent snow
                    covering our beds

as we drift into a deep well
                    of waiting.

<16>

MARCH

Some effort's required to realize winter
        coats can't yet be put away,
even if my neighbor's considering early planting.

Squirrels shiver, look askance
        at the way wind whips
naked trees making me wonder about why

a lone robin perches in the bare branches
        of the Chinese maple tree in my yard.

She's been there for about an hour —
I admire her red breast as the sun strikes noon,

then I lose myself in the newspaper only to check again
        to observe if she is still there.

Yes — not yet frozen — just waiting somewhat dismayed
        that the trip north was too soon.

I make a sandwich, brew a cup of herbal tea,
        wonder if I will have to scrape
ice from the windshield in the morning.

Hours later she's still there — ruffled and squatting,
        immobile and steadfast;
should I offer her some bread crumbs?

Better suited for this chill, she won't fly away
        just because it's not what she expected.

<17>

APRIL

Spring's holding back this year
like my hands,
        thrust in jacket pockets,
too cold to touch the doorknob
to the shed where the garden tools
        wait in semi-darkness,
dusty with winter's sullen breath.

Grass seeds flung
        on barren patches of lawn
        offer uncertain designs that
may or may not emerge as new blades.
A chill rain drips down
        the windowpane:
        a perfect day for reading.

As I follow others' words
        sliding across stark white pages,
        thoughts, ideas unfold
faster than forsythia buds against the stone
        wall where the peonies push
        damp dirt aside:

creatures from another world, where waiting
        for the right moment can be either
liberating or fatal, depending on the fickleness
        of each unstable day,
unaware of my cold hands
        turning another page to discover
another question or partial answer.

<18>

MAY

Sandwiched between uncertain April
and sunny June,
                    May makes demands —
pay attention to beginnings, endings:
last day of school,
                    summer vacation.
Warm weather tempts us to take risks.
After plowing the garden, my father
              sets seedlings to harvest
                    in months to come.
I've turned in my band uniform,
              dusted off the croquet set,
arranged the hoops in the side yard:
                    tournaments begin next week.
There's a sense of discovery
              hidden behind every new leaf.
On Memorial Day
              my aunt asks me to help her
plant geraniums at the cemetery.
We place several on ancestors'
                         resting places;
she saves one fading flower for
a child's grave with a lamb on the stone:
                    no name, no date.

<19>

She stares at me and says:
                    this is my stillborn son.
I knew about him, but she thought I didn't;
In her eyes a void —
                    she looks beyond me,
                    beyond the tilted stones,
to days ended before they began.

<20>

June

Stillness in Chardin's painting:
strawberries picked,
placed in a graceful conical arrangement,
                    untouchable but to the eye.

Finding just the right
                elements to combine, he chose
two white carnations, beside a glass of water,
            a peach, two red cherries.

Bringing summer inside,
            he creates a rustic table to contemplate.

The local church celebrates the season
            with a noisy festival
                    of strawberries and cream —

How would he interpret
            noisy children dashing about,
women in aprons with plastic cups and spoons,
            dishing out the sugared desserts
            to people eating from paper plates?

I remember when I was ten, the firemen's
            Strawberry Festival in the yard
                across from our house —
I wanted a dish of whipped cream, fresh berries;
            but my parents liked fruit in a bowl
            on the kitchen table.

<21>

JULY

Month of water lilies —
      Monet's garden at Giverny
blooms in museums — large canvases
      surpassing all impressionist
paintings, inviting us to enter
      a watery world of blurred colors:
blue, purple, green, yellow — all free-floating.
Monet said: *Perhaps I owe it to flowers*
      for having become a painter.
My parents' garden,
      framed with zinnias,
shades of the rainbow, planted as a border
to peas, potatoes, cabbage, peppers, onions
and ripening tomatoes,
shimmered in
      sweltering summer.
Weeks of ninety degrees, burning sun created
      sleepless nights. I made a
bed on the back porch,
      and in moonlight as I fell asleep,
I heard flowers singing in harmony
      to each other, in French,
wishing Monet
      could see them, paint them
in his garden of dreams.

<22>

AUGUST

A humid day,
         sweltering, unforgiving —
I'm picking ripe tomatoes,
               some split with heat,
               juice oozing,
               seeds seeping out.
Red-winged black
               bird flashes
               by the porch,
darts to a branch in the pine tree.
My mother's in the kitchen,
         slicing vegetables for beef stew.
Red-winged blackbird flies
to porch gutter,
searches for water.
Mid-afternoon blaze of sun,
                  I'm restless, on edge.
I hear a shot
            across the street, then silence.
Red-winged blackbird
               freezes on the clothesline.
Locked in his room,
               my cousin
                     shot himself.
I drop the basket of tomatoes.

<23>

My mother's at the screen door,
holding a stirring spoon.

Red-winged blackbird soars
over the roof into the sky.

<24>

SEPTEMBER

A few leaves on the Oak trees tinged with red —
morning chill lingers;
children trudge to school,

weighted down with book bags
musical instruments,
weariness of the coming day.

I remember fourth grade —
Mrs. Elliott's project to create
a Native American village in miniature.

We gathered moss, sand, twigs,
wove tiny blankets,
sculpted clay figures.

Just as leaves continued to fall,
I began to lose interest in wigwams.

Then one afternoon, picking the last tomatoes,
I found an arrowhead
in the furrow of our garden.

That night I dreamt about feathers
on a head dress, peering in my window:
I heard soft footsteps
outside — the crunch of dry leaves
woke me to an eerie silence.

<25>

Next day the street was littered with
                    more reminders of fall
as I walked to school grasping
          the arrowhead in my pocket.

<26>

OCTOBER

Leaves clog the gutters
        whoever cleans them is late.
Small annoyances tip the afternoon into evening.

I wait for rain.

Eventually everything needs attention:
not just clogged drains
        but my muddled misunderstandings
 of how the spin of the earth
        brings whirlwinds,
lapping around the house
making the sound of a huge tongue
        licking the moldings
sticking its tip into the door frame
        tasting the solitude.

I know the rain is coming.

Cardinals shiver in bushes,
edges of leaves turn up,
some in despair as it's October.

Thunder in the distance —
        should I make a try at cleaning
the gutters?
        No listen, I'm not willing.

<27>

Yes it's raining;
        water's trickling through windows.
I stand here watching
a minor flood from the drains.

<28>

November

Strands of bronze,
                    gold dancing leaves
swirl over the street's surface:
spinning,
          whirling,
                    twisting
to unheard music: the wind's symphony.

Trees shake their few dry leaves:
                    leaflets from angry protesters,
messages raked into piles or blown away.

Grey clouds push down
                    against the hills,
threatening rain — could be snow.

If there were a secluded rift,
          I would slide through to solitude.

5:30 p.m.

Darkness holds us in its grip:
          we're saving time — but for what —
Longer evenings,
                    earlier sunrises?

<29>

Does the day make sense to birds,
        especially ones who lack intuition
                to fly to a warmer place?
And those dancing leaves —
are they aware the music ends?

<30>

DECEMBER

A lone jogger in a black hooded jacket,
a determined monk,
                    runs for salvation;
salt stained cars slide through stop sign
                        at twelfth street.

We have reached the moment of hesitation
where winter hovers and fall surrenders.

Trees reveal bare skeletons against grey sky,
                    pointing to shapes in clouds.

Dark December follows me into the house.

In the middle ages by candle light,
Irish monks copied texts in winter,
drawing swirling
                    designs, decorating words.
How did they warm their hands?
Some wrote personal poems in the margins:
                    fables or forbidden lyrics.

In a warm kitchen my mother ladles
alphabet soup — I try to form a word in
                    the broth before I taste it.

<31>

It's December 9th — my father's uneasy about
   headlines that make him nervous.

Dark December follows me
               throughout the night.

<32>

THE
DAYS

MONDAY

This morning my neighbor arrives
with a plastic container of wild
blackberries, picked in the gully
hidden behind his house.

I'm reading Chekhov's story,
"Gooseberries," about a lazy
Russian estate owner who lies
in bed all day eating his favorite

gooseberries which he planted,
to secure his happiness;
to others they taste bitter —
he deludes himself.

My neighbor tells me to add
Cool Whip, but they are sour —
tastes differ — the week begins
with silent compromise.

<35>

TUESDAY

This morning the window washer
wakes me at 8 a.m. squishing his
agitator, thumping his ladder
against the side of the house.

Rain's forecast for today so his
efforts are a bit misplaced.

I make the effort to fix breakfast —
instant oatmeal — peaches and cream —
rather dry in the bowl —
a product of space travel food.

I wonder if the paper delivery
hit the porch without crashing
into the flowers? Yes, good shot —
here's *The Times'* plastic blue wrapper.

The lawn crew arrives with their
instruments of torture — a grinding
mower, a roaring leaf-blower.
Even the cat retreats to the closet —
this day forebodes no rest.

<36>

WEDNESDAY

Just as I was settling down to read
the morning paper, I heard a rush
of water in the kitchen. Yesterday,
the cold water wouldn't turn off, so
I found a lever under the sink, shut it off —
a feat for me. But now the hot water
gushes full force; I can't locate the
off lever — only after several minutes
I find it behind the works
of the garbage disposal, hidden.
Bruce, the plumber, is set to arrive
around noon with a new faucet,
a new lease on life. I decide to read
a few poems by W. S. Merwin:
Bill Moyers interviewed him on PBS
last evening; they discussed "Yesterday"
a poem about men not taking time
to talk to their fathers until it is too
late — I wonder if I missed the chance
to say something to my Dad but
can't think of anything that he would
have wanted to hear, unless I recounted
my problems with the plumbing.

<37>

Rocks everywhere. From a dug-up sewer,
my neighbors arrange them for a garden:
some too heavy to carry need a wheelbarrow.
I have a large pink-and-grey rock for
a doorstop — its origins a mystery;
it never responds when struck or pushed.
On my desk a round white rock from
Walden Pond, picked up on the shore
near the site of Thoreau's cabin.
When I feel the edges, slight grooves,
I think of him sitting in the cold,
looking out over the pond,
himself solid in his solitude.
Shakespeare's Macbeth said
Stones have been known to move.
What if all these stones were alive
to express how they experience
the world, how to live, survive?
I put Thoreau's stone back on my desk;
it holds down many written words
not yet read, waiting to be spoken.

<38>

FRIDAY

◇————◇

Early this morning mulch arrives
        on my neighbor's driveway:
        I google "mulch": *a mixture of decaying*
        organic substances spread as fertilizer.
They shovel the compost around
        flowers and shrubs,
        a full day's work with no letup.
I'm struggling with how to begin
        a poem about birds, how they
        consume bread crumbs —
starlings push other birds around,
        jump from one crumb to another,
unable to decide — they have
        yellow rings around their eyes:
pirates stealing, hoarding,
        helping only themselves.
Spreading mulch continues
        most of the day: the mystery of
        making plants grow puzzles me:
my droopy petunias, infested
        with bugs, have lacy leaves,
        an unhealthy sign.
I think about how
        mulch came to be — someone ground
        up plants, manure, compounds
        making nature respond —
I notice a chipmunk eating one last
        crumb — he's oblivious to the birds,
mulch, flowers, scampering into his hole.

<39>

SATURDAY

Saws grinding. Limbs crashing down.
In the street behind me, men working —
one in a cherry picker high in the branches.

Another tree dismembered for safety,
but from what? Crushing a roof —
dragging down a live wire — always
some danger lurking in the wind.

The Oak tree in the front of my house
rebels, sending its roots through
the sidewalks, cracking cement,
twisting around its trunk,
a prehistoric sea creature,
trying to break free of a trap.

Finally, the buzzing stops: lunch
break, then the final severing,
toting away, like battlefield
casualties, unidentified and lost.

<40>

SUNDAY

After a sleepless night I scan the day
with few prospects of making sense
of the night storm flooding my neighbor's
fish pond. Most of his exotic species
did not survive, swept over the side,
tossed into the gully behind his house.
Were any of his fish sleeping? Yes, fish sleep,
don't close their eyes, find a dark crevice
at the bottom, slow down metabolism,
get energy for the next day. Do they dream
about meeting another fish, finding food,
discovering new fish faces or being caught?
Maybe they are like my computer going
to "sleep"— just waiting for someone
to make contact, need amusement,
or check to see if they still can swim,
or if they float to the surface, dead weight.

<41>

THE
HOURS

MORNING

Spoon tossed
on granite counter

spotted by sunlight

cracked teacup
bordered with pale poppies

sunlight on granite counter
chipped saucer

once part of a service
for six: spoons, cups, saucers

outside the kitchen window
disagreeable crows

negotiate among
the dogwood tree blossoms

twisted napkin beside
the teacup, pale poppies

sunlight on crows
half-opened blossoms

<45>

MID-MORNING

wasp clings
to the kitchen curtain

crawling inch by inch

curtain blows in wind
wasp keeps crawling, clinging

reflection on granite counter
orange sliver on chipped plate

once part of a dozen: now divided

wasp circles granite counter
lands on orange sliver

ignores curtains/wind
dives into orange slice/juice

napkin untwisted
beside saucer, teacup

overcast, wind, drizzle
through open window

wasp immovable
on chipped saucer/pale poppies

dog howls
at shadow in trees

<46>

NOON

Dining-room clock
wound daily, strikes twelve

resonates to kitchen

where dead wasp
floats in juice from orange

window open, soft rain
curtains graze granite counter

water on cracked cup
with pale poppies

last of the set of six
forgotten gift in sink

soaped/rinsed/drying

twelve chimes unwind
another hour vanishes

damp breeze, dust rises
on granite counter

<47>

wasp motionless
faucet drips

spoon slips to floor
clouds gather, wind increases

dog growls

<48>

MID-AFTERNOON

windows grow dim
wind buffets, swirls

no sunlight on twisted napkin

wasp drowns
in sweet, enticing juice

outside, sycamore tree
bends, branches buckle

leaves twitch, float free

clock once ticked: no longer
chiming/hands frozen

rain through open
window, damp curtains,

spatters granite counter
stained with dust, dirt,

leaves fly, scatter
float in sink, swirl

around saucer, pale poppies

a whirlpool —
wasp swept into sink

<49>

EARLY EVENING

Cicadas grind in sycamore
tree, dark clouds, brisk wind

bits of broken branches

strike window, fall on sill
granite counter now littered

leaves in a pool of juice
crust of bread/jelly

beside a flickering candle

crows in dogwood tree
dispute no longer

jockey for limbs
feathers, wet wings flap

folded napkin soiled with jelly
faucet dripping, dripping

candle burns out, darkness
crows leap from branch to branch

wind whips leaves, dogwood blossoms
sycamore tree shivers

no dog howls

<50>

EVENING

Streetlight beams
strike granite counter

windowsill drenched
leaves litter the sink

car's headlights flash
above granite counter

a beetle, brown and sticky
emerges from a crack

intent on food
senses jelly, a bread crust

cicadas cease, crows silent
darkness settles sound

napkin next to burnt-out match
jelly stain/outline of orange slice

siren shrieks, blue, red,
lights flash in all corners

no wasp, only puddles

<51>

no clock ticking
water drips on pale poppies

sleeping beetle
bread crust

edge of the moon

<52>

MIDNIGHT

wasp's wing floats in water

water dripping still
on cracked cup, saucer, poppies

dining-room clock rewound
strikes twelve, echoes in kitchen

streetlight out, candle flickers
crows lost in blackness

beetle immobile, satiated
darkness everywhere

littered leaves float in sink
half-eaten bread crust discarded

cicadas damp, quiet
on split branches of sycamore

dog rattles chain
howls at red, burning moon

toads leap in wet grass
celebrating

<53>

THE PAST IS
A COUNTRY
WITH NO BORDERS

ONE SECOND

the past is a country with no borders
requiring no passport

no maps give directions
with no street signs I'm lost

traveling down an endless road
names and addresses don't exist

shadows hover around me
I hear voices but see no faces

time makes no difference here
today and yesterday the same

yet I travel here with chosen words
arranged to recreate a place

where I escape the several selves
of my layered existence

memories slide into each other
shifting plates beneath the earth

both frightening and welcoming
mirrored in an extended line

I'm searching for the moment
a single second to light up the sky

<57>

IN THE SHADOWS

I was six and wanted to be alone —
I would hide in the shadows under

the forsythia bush, watching the praying
mantis circling an oak leaf above,

tracing an outline, waiting to devour
an unsuspecting fly or spider.

Or I would crawl under the front porch
and gaze through lattice work

at strollers, dog walkers or joggers,
stepping over cracks and fallen branches.

At Sunday dinner I hid under the table;
the lace cloth created a shaded tent.

I knew the family by their familiar shoes:
Dad's dress Florsheims, Aunt Bessie's

patent-leather pumps, Grandma's laced-
up brogans, tying all of us together.

<58>

The gloom hidden inside troubled me:
fear that I would grow up not knowing

what kind of shoes would fit me
or if I could walk through a crowd

without panic, feeling as safe
as one who no longer needed shadows.

<59>

END OF OCTOBER

1.

Brisk evenings, dry leaves crunching
on the street — pumpkin cutting time.

Mother complained about the mess
in the kitchen when I sliced

out a face: jagged teeth, triangle
for a nose, diamond-shaped eyes.

A candle flickered in his face,
glowing in the front window.

I was ten. He was my sinister twin
to scare away witches, evil spirits.

<60>

2.

But next door an old man died —
mother blew out the candle.

Viewing the corpse laid out
in his house, I knelt on the bench

in front of the casket;
two candles, one on each side,

cast a somber glow —
his hand grasped his rosary.

I wondered if he now knew
spirits were abroad this night.

<61>

3.

Mother cut up the jack-o'-lantern
sliced and mashed the pulp,

mixed dough and rolled out
a pie crust — her specialty,

slid my twin into the oven,
baked a dessert (not for me).

I carried it with regret
to the unsuspecting family.

Outside trick-or-treat voices
rang through the street.

<62>

THE BIRDWOMAN

1.

In fourth grade
I read about Lewis and Clark,
exploring woods,
crossing rivers,
making camps,
meeting guides,
surviving weather.

A Shoshone woman,
Sacajawea, hired as a translator,
traveled with her husband and son,
knew many secrets. She spoke to birds
read signs in the sky, found trails to nowhere.

2.

In our town Ava lived
by the water tower
on a hill in a small house,
a sanctuary for finches,
canaries, parakeets
in cages near the windows.
Every day she trekked
to the general store
for bird seed,
passed the school carrying
a pack on her back,
her legs bent, her eyes on the ground.

<63>

3.

We called her Sacajawea,
the mysterious Birdwoman.
If we got close to her house,
we could hear her singing,
talking to her birds.
Once we saw feathers
in her hair. Seeds floated in the air.
No one had been in her house.

4.

We made a map of Lewis and Clark's
travels: a long twisting line
over several states.
All but one of his explorers survived.
Sacajawea suffered physical pain
survived hardships,
gave up her son to be educated,
died on the reservation.

<64>

5.

Ava's loneliness
expanded through morning fog:
one day the birds' songs
ceased. She opened cages,
windows, set them free.
A bright green parakeet
flew past the classroom window.

No one witnessed her leaving,
I pictured her in the pages
of my history book:
a proud falcon fastening
claws on a bare branch.

<65>

POPPIES

November eleventh, fifth grade —
    we recite a poem in unison:
    "In Flanders Field the Poppies Grow,"
pause after key lines, stress important words:
    We are the Dead and *We shall not sleep.*

Voices evoking the Great War:
    I'm confused, don't understand
about rows of crosses marking places
    with poppies growing in the field,
        larks flying "amid the guns below."

My teacher gives us silk poppies with four
    petals, from The American Legion;
    we drop our coins in a slot
in a can with a red-white-and-blue label:
    Honor Their Service.

As I walk home, with the poppy pinned
    to my shirt, a line runs through my
    head: *we throw the torch* —
how are we to catch it — flying through the air —
    how to hold it high?

In the sky, Flanders Field emerges from clouds;
    silent birds hover over crosses,
    thousands of poppies swirl in the wind,
blood-red patterns with a life of their own
    unlike those who will never see them.

<66>

BAKING DAY

My mother cracks eggs, pours the yolks
into the round circle of flour, stirs, mixes soft dough.

Rolled out like a big pancake, sliced into thin
strips, noodles dry over backs of kitchen chairs.

I go to the A&P for two items: sugar & more flour
for rhubarb pie: red stalks with fan
      like poisonous leaves.

The sidewalk to the store has weathered many years.
I step over cracks not to fall through
      to some strange place.

At the A&P Mr. Archie looks down over the counter; he has
a long pole with pincers, grasps boxes, swings them down.

On my way back I remember Aunt Thelma saying Uncle
Frank was *cracked*. Was he split like the eggs
      or the sidewalk?

When I came into the kitchen, the pie pan was greased,
rhubarb sliced; my mother sat by the window
      lost in thought.

<67>

I asked about being *cracked:* she mixed the sugar & flour, said,
"Not *right in the noodle* or *half baked*":
       not like her dough or pie.

<68>

ARROWHEAD

In soft rain
I see his shadow
under pine trees
stepping over stones
that speak in whispers

Twigs snap
a squirrel breathes
a narrow stream stops flowing

I float toward the fine drizzle

The arrowhead
a stone carved to a point
designed to kill
shines in the dark

I found it in the furrow
of a freshly plowed
garden among pieces
of pottery   shards of glass

I feel the sharp edges

The hunter waits
searching for his
lost weapon
in the underbrush

<69>

I place it on the window
sill in the moonlight
wait for his touch
a glimpse of feathers

<70>

JOURNEYS

1.

After reading *The Odyssey*
in seventh grade,
I wanted a bed
like Odysseus'
with posts of tree
trunks, unmovable,
growing from the ground
through the floor.
Penelope and he
knew the secret.

I told my father
about the tree-bed;
I recounted Odysseus'
journeys,
the need to get home,
how his son didn't know him,
how he wanted Penelope
to recognize him,
trust him.

My father said, "Let me work this out."

<71>

2.

That summer,
in the Maple tree
in our backyard we built
a tree house with a board floor,
several spaces for branches
to grow and twine through.
It had open sides
and a partial roof
to keep out rain.

When I climbed the ladder
unrolled my sleeping bag
under the shifting leaves,
I could touch the stars
shining on the Aegean.
Odysseus answered the riddle
of the bed. It could not be moved.

All was calm. We knew.

<72>

OPEN WINDOW, 1942

Sheer curtains wave in a soft breeze,
        I practice Chopin's *Minute Waltz;*

I knew about Chopin's death: body buried in Paris —
        his sister transported his heart to Warsaw.

I focus on lines of the staff, they are train tracks —
        notes like cars, returning his heart home.

I continue to play his composition,
weary of the quickening pace, wonder about time.

When a cool breeze stimulates my playing,
I choose a *Polonaise,* a dance to cheer my spirits.

I feel Chopin's shadow and heart-beats in the melody,
        notes dance proudly on the tracks.

An unexpected whirlwind sweeps music
      from my piano —
I fear an approaching storm, close the window,

not knowing other trains in Poland rush into darkness
with passengers facing the last minutes of heart-beats...

<73>

Almost Twelve

1.

Climbing a tree is easy: my feet and legs
wrap round the trunk, cling to high branches;

floating in space, I feel the coolness of autumn:
where are all those noisy birds?

Leaves flame on the Maples, drop one by one,
cover the front yard like paper cutouts:

trees tell me: we are tired — we are cold;
understand we're changing.

I rake piles of red, yellow, brown, bronze;
bury myself in a heap of dry crunchiness.

2.

Next morning my father wakes me from
a dream of shivering trees, swirling leaves.

With no ceremony we drag the bundles
to the back yard where the flames

simmer, glow, then blaze red hot,
consuming the mounds: the leaves roar.

<74>

3.

Almost twelve: too old to climb trees,
too young to grasp the allurement of fire.

In my mind trees' branches burst forth
with summer leaves, shelter birds.

Now days are shorter: what happened to eleven?
Why does the spiraling smoke smart,

hurt my eyes: what should I know? Tell me,
tell me how to understand the ashes.

<75>

MUSIC LESSON

A rainy April afternoon,
    tomorrow is my thirteenth birthday:

I walk to my piano teacher's house,
    thinking about my cake,
    German chocolate,
my mother's specialty.

His house is silent; his dog greets
    me at the door.

Seated at the piano, I wait for instructions:
he says: "Play the Chopin waltz, again."

    I touch the keys.

Something strange happens:
    rain against the windows;
    darkness creeps into the room.

Notes float off the page,
    circle my head,
dance against the ceiling and doors.

Striking the last note,

I notice he's standing at the window,
    gazing at his garden.

<76>

I thought he said: "My flowers weep."

But maybe it was "Showers all week," or
        "Same time next week."

He stands with his back
            to me, staring at rain.

I leave behind another year,
    open the door for the spring breeze.

<77>

CARDS

Sunday afternoons my Dad and uncle
teach me various card games:

Go Fish, Authors, and Old Maid.
(Discard matching pairs — loser gets the old Maid).

Often I win against them — except for Old Maid —
I get stuck with her again and again.

The only real old maids I know
are two sisters, Maud and Mable Meade,
who live down the street.

They go everywhere together;
my Dad says: *they are joined at the hip* —
(I don't think so as I see them at separate times,
feeding their seven cats on their back porch).

When I lose a game, Dad says:
You will have to go and live with them.

So the usual Sunday game begins
with Dad and uncle having good luck;
they have all the pairs — I get stuck
with the Old Maid five times.

Then I notice the corner of the card
is marked with a small black dot.

They are cheating!

<78>

In anger I upset the card table
tear up the card
                run to my room shouting
I'm going to live with the old maids' cats.

I hear the pair of them laughing.

<79>

CROQUET

summer games on the lawn —
wooden balls hit through wire hoops
or wickets — the goal — reach a painted stake
at the end of the playing field

we strike with wooden mallets to maneuver
through intricate patterns —
if we thwack another player's ball

we propel it across the grass

a noisy game

cracking of wood against wood —
winning makes a summer day even better

later we learn of other hoops and wickets

some to restrict us
some to jump through
some to outwit us
some to end the game

sunny afternoons gone —

striking toward winning stakes
requires more than skill with a mallet

new opponents don't play by the same rules

<80>

TREE-TALK

I hear tapping
at my bedroom window
I crouch under covers
alone in the dark
wondering
if someone outside
wants to come in

The tree by the window
often talks to me
in the morning
whispering
get up and see
the sun rise
the sky turn blue
hear the birds
in my leaves

But could this be
the same tree
anxious to be heard
at night
with wind whipping
its bare branches
wanting me
to open the window
and listen

<81>

I toss off the blanket
cross the carpet
to the closed window
raise the frame
but all is silent
the tree waits
the moon filters
through a few last leaves

<82>

AFTER THE RAIN

Today, my father says, *Get in the car*;
    we drive to a place new to me,
stop in front of a house I don't recognize.

Rain's everywhere — on the roof, in the gutters,
    streaming down sidewalks.
We don't have an umbrella — hurry inside.

Rooms are dark — blinds are lowered.
    My father ushers my two aunts
to the kitchen, tells them to keep quiet.

In a small room my grandfather lies in a coffin —
    I've never seen him before.
Neither has spoken to the other for twenty years.

My father takes my hand, leads me to the corpse —
    says: *This is my father who did not like boys,
hurt me, took me out of school to work in the mines.*

He lifts the thin veil covering the body,
    stares, says: *I want you to touch him.*
He places my hand on his father's cold hand.

I don't know what to say or what to think —
    how could someone who was never
alive to me be dead — be lying peacefully.

<83>

Rain belts against the window —
My father says, *Now he can never touch you
as he touched me — we are both free.*

My aunts burst into the room with angry
            voices, telling my father
to leave, not to come back — go into the storm.

As we walk down the sidewalk, the shower stops —
      I jump in the biggest puddle, splash
both my father and me as I run to the car.

<84>

BREAKFAST

through the cold I hear my Dad's voice
urging me to get up or I'll be late

there is no central heating in the house
he rises early to build a fire in the stove

then cooks his breakfast — fried bread
and cheese with a fried egg on top

when I dash for the bathroom I can smell
the odors of toasting bread, melting cheese

there is a gas stove next to the sink
and tub, but Mom's afraid that if I light it

an explosion might send the claw-foot tub
and toilet with a wooden seat sailing

through the wall with the towels and
soap — what would the neighbors think about

how we live — so I shiver and wash my face
and hurry downstairs to avoid more warnings

every morning we go through the same ritual
do I want bread, cheese and an egg

and I refuse, wanting stale cake in a bowl
of milk, watching the icing float

<85>

then the door slams, my Dad's gone
I'm left alone in a slowly warming kitchen

with thoughts about why we are so
different and why I can't go back to bed

<86>

FLAMES

As a kid burning refuse in a large garbage can
gave me a thrill
      imagining
      myself an heroic agent
assigned to explode an enemy stronghold
I was the sinister fireman
      who struck the match igniting
a cracker-box house
but time passed and I found fire in other places

In the fall after leaf-raking and gathering
broken branches
      we built a fire in the garden
      now cleared of stubble
roasted hot dogs on a stick
as flames rose higher
      like red and yellow waves
I danced around the pyre
like a primitive chief chanting ancient rites

Aunt Carrie who taught Sunday school
worried about my not knowing
      about heaven and hell
      described the devil
all red and glowing from eternal fire
tempting sinners so he could sweep them
      into a flaming pit forever
I didn't accept her story
but enjoyed eating her apple pie

<87>

Later in literature class we read Dante's *Inferno*
inhabitants of hell were in a bad way
  so many methods to punish sinners
  so many famous names
in Canto 26 I read about Ulysses, a hero trapped
forever in fire speaking from the tip of a flame
    punished for lying
   giving false counsel to his men
I realized being a hero had its limitations

<88>

WALKERS

On my street I watch walkers with dogs:
a retired administrator whose Cavalier Spaniel

wants a stomach rub — the slim woman who rescues
retired racing Greyhounds, leads three on one leash;

an unknown intruder who never picks up after
his Great Dane who deposits unwanted reminders.

When I was a kid, I hid behind the porch railing,
watching the street for our town's wanderers:

the war veteran with one useless, swinging arm,
who liked to scare us by waving his crutch;

the red-nosed lawyer, a drinker who staggered
home early, leaning against Oak trees;

an eccentric bird woman who had fifteen
parakeets, making many trips to the store for feed.

At night I watched out my bedroom window
for prowlers and thieves, creeping out of my books:

Captain Hook and company, singing sea shanties;
Dracula drooling with his black cape flying;

the Witch from Snow White with a bag
full of red apples, tempting all the neighbors.

<89>

On nightly walks in my neighborhood
I watch for uneven, patched sidewalks,

step aside for bright oncoming head lights,
with discretion peer into lighted windows.

I slow down my pace and follow my shadow,
number stars, stop to measure the moon.

<90>

CHIMES

I couldn't sleep
it was my first time
away from home

my aunt made the couch
a bed with a home
made quilt

she went to bed early
the room was dark
the clock chimed

every fifteen minutes
not just one bell but
a whole song

I couldn't sleep
the bells rang out
time passing

at home the dining
room clock struck
the hours

only once in awhile
did I hear them
from my bedroom

<91>

I missed my dog lying
at the foot of my bed
the silence of my room

so this is what visiting
another home was like
not comfortable at all

in the morning my aunt
got up early and brewed
coffee which I didn't like

she had firm ideas
made me eat eggs
and bacon for breakfast
when at home I liked
milk and cereal
toast with jam

my aunt insisted I brush
my teeth twice
take a shower

I usually just rolled
out of bed put on my
worn T-shirt and jeans

<92>

the clock kept chiming
every fifteen minutes
I was losing patience

when she asked me if I
was having a good time
I had to nod yes and smile

why my parents wanted
me to visit my aunt
confused me

I was eager to get
home to my dog
my cluttered room

away from the fifteen
minute reminders of my aunt
jangling in my ears

<93>

RITUAL ROCK

under the chokeberry tree
I find a rock

I see embedded
on its side a leaf

not a chokeberry one
but a delicate fern

I hold the rock
close to my ear

it whispers strange
ritual words

I hear drum-beats
swish of feathers

jangle of bracelets
rattle of tinkling bells

chants evoking spirits
praising the earth

<94>

I imagine the rock
hidden in my book bag

but know I must not
disturb the delicate balance

even though I cherish
this link to another world

<95>

WORDS

My mother enjoyed conversations:
neighbors dropped in often;
her brother stopped for a shot of whiskey —
the bottle hidden in the cupboard.

Talking filled our house — I was the listener.
I struggled to understand all the words.

At bedtime my mother read me my favorite story,
    "Rip Van Winkle."
I thought his name was "wrinkle" as he was old,
      slept most of his life away.
His wife talked all the time — he didn't miss her.

To remind us of our duties, my father said few words.

Once I asked him to read me the same story;
      as he turned the pages,
I realized the words he spoke were unfamiliar;
      when I protested, he got angry,
slammed the book shut and left the bedroom.

Later I discovered his secret and shame;
      he couldn't read very many sentences;
      he didn't know the story of "Rip Van Winkle;"
he never bought me a book or wrote me a letter,
      never admitted words were strangers.

<96>

NIGHTCRAWLERS

The yard changes shape with the light from the porch;
      which excites and energizes my father
who announces: *let's look for nightcrawlers.*

I never went fishing with my father who loved the river;
      he would sit on the front steps anticipating
how he would show off his catch of the day.

Years wear away the need for connections as he bends
      down in the moonlight to touch the grass;
why did he think the earth would reject its blanket?

Yes, it comes back — we would dig holes —
      wait for the bait,
collect them in a can — I squirmed at their presence —
they are still there under the grass; he doesn't
      want them now.

The light from the kitchen window makes
      a glowing rectangle
which reminds him of his safe place;
he knows his limitations, hesitates to catch fish
      for others.

<97>

THE KINGFISHER

Those long
summer nights
when I couldn't
sleep
I thought about
where I could fly.

Once I became
an exotic bird
spreading
graceful wings
diving
into a deep pond
catching fish.

With each splash
I breathed deeper
rose to the surface
the catch
mounting
beside the bed.

In the morning
the room
smelled
of scales
on the floor
wet
footprints.

<98>

FIELDS

a seven-year-old boy with light brown hair
watches over me or waits inside me

many times I dream about him as he walks
down a cobblestone street on a bright

morning in a small French village just
as the sun rises and a delivery wagon

drawn by a white horse stops and waits
at doorsteps while milk is poured into

pitchers for the sleepy villagers who
open their shutters for the fresh air

he doesn't speak but gestures to a just
cut golden field of hay in the distance

I wonder why he is awake so early
or what he wants to tell me

last week as I lay drifting into a haze
for surgery the same seven-year-old

boy with light brown hair runs through
a field of lavender waving in the breeze

the soft purples bathed in bright light
are alluring calming enticing

<99>

he chases several white butterflies
all part of his joyful summer game

in a nearby field the sunflowers
spread in straight rows to the horizon

he points to them and smiles
a gesture of how to touch the sky

<100>

Rain

1.

A child sits by a window
staring at rain beating
against the pane,
reading a story
about a small boy
caught in a thunderstorm
with no umbrella
or raincoat.
Words on the page
melt and drip down
onto the floor:
he believes his chair is a boat —
floats to the ceiling,
doesn't know how to swim.

<101>

2.

In the schoolroom
the teacher fears rain
creeping under the cracked door,
rising to the chalkboard,
washing away her written
words about a boy reading
a book in a boat.
She orders the students
to stand on desks —
they refuse, want to swim
have a holiday.
She wades to the window,
jumps from the ledge
flies away.

<102>

3.

An elderly woman hears
cold water dripping in her kitchen,
leaking through the roof.
She puts a newspaper
over her head — the obituary
column soaks through;
she sits at the breakfast
table — her tea cup overflows
into a puddle where a small
boy reading a book,
paddling in a boat,
calls out for help.
She has never saved
anyone's life.

<103>

4.

Cloudbursts at the cemetery
muddy the grave — mourners
huddle in a soggy tent.
Lightning flashes;
thunder roars,
drowning the minister's
prayer to the heavens.
The boat shaped casket
sinks into the ground.
Words float to the surface.
An elderly woman
weeps for the drowned
boy who can't swim,
who reads too many books.

<104>

Shadows on the Wall

Late afternoon — strange sunlight
     filters through the window,
casts shadows of leaves and branches
     on the kitchen wall:
grey to black the images hover,
     linger for several minutes.

On each leaf dark silhouettes
     fade and reappear speaking
silent words floating from leaf to leaf —
     I don't recognize the faces
or make sense of why they want to speak
     as light grows dimmer.

I listen to voices from the dark shadows
     as if leaves have stories to relay —
Am I connected to the life of the tree?
     As the light fades,
I am left with my own shadow,
     voiceless as a fallen leaf.

<105>

ECHOES
OF TIME

THE SENSE OF INTERNAL TIME

From my bedroom I listen for the Seth Thomas
        clock downstairs on the mantle to strike —
I silently count, knowing that twelve o'clock
        signals another day —

The ancient time-piece strikes every hour —
        my mother insists my father
should be named after the clock — he's always
        on time, never misses a meal.

My father insists on Swiss efficiency,
        wears an imposing wrist watch,
which he often consults to remind us
        to be efficient and not late.

I wonder if all the Swiss are so addicted
        to watches, to accuracy; I find out
in Bern when I visit with a Swiss friend
        a seven-hundred-year-old clock tower.

In the town square it chimes at noon, displays
        astrological signs, carved figures
parade with a crowing rooster, reminding
        everyone of memories of the past.

Just observe your wrist, watch the second-hand
        circle and glide past the numbers,
the heart beats, the breath comes and goes,
        taking us to other times and places.

<109>

BLUE JAY

afternoons unfold as a day or a few seconds
a leaf just turning or a series of clocks striking

my last visit provokes my aunt who keeps
her mother from the world she knows

my grandmother avoids wearing
a watch or accepting a season

there is no time to lead a new life
for her last months in a strange house

I arrive from my first year at college
comment about cloudy weather

she asks: *do you notice how sun shines
through maple leaves — they turn gold*

outside, a blue jay insists the day is his
but the feeder is empty

my aunt lights a cigarette in the next room
smoke snakes through the doorway

<110>

STRAWBERRIES

1.

Home for lunch in sixth grade
Smucker twins on the table
peanut butter and strawberry
jam — mother butters bread
I get plates, pour milk
bite into the sandwich
pure pleasure —
mother wears an old apron
patterned with fruit and vines
made for her by her mother.

2.

Tenth-grade infatuation
she loves chocolate-covered
strawberries — I thaw frozen ones
dip them in melted Hershey bars
wrap them in red tissue paper —
a Valentine's Day gift
left in her locker —
inside a love note about
how I want to meet her —
she never responds.

<111>

3.

In college studying *Othello*
I read about Desdemona's
magical handkerchief
embroidered with strawberries
ensuring her lover's loyalty
but when lost, evokes damnation
her virtue tainted —
I read with dread
Iago's schemes to trick
Othello to doubt his wife —
alas, he smothers her.

4.

Office-party midsummer's eve
strawberries dipped in sugar
served with champagne
older woman entices me to dance
old song in my head —
Casey waltzes with the strawberry
blonde — his mind nearly explodes
she shakes with alarm —
no fear or hesitation here
she desires to lead — the band plays on.

<112>

5.

Three a.m. I toss, turn can't sleep
problems swirl — in my head
tape repeats the day's routine —
I long for fresh strawberries
slip into the kitchen
fill a bowl with rich cream
savor my favorite fruit —
echoes of my mother's voice
I hope you enjoy your dessert
I am ten years old again.

<113>

NEST

a bird's building a nest
in the transom over my front door

debris scattered on the porch
twigs   hair   twine

why choose this unlikely place
when trees surround

this is no place to set up house-
keeping to nurture young

I climb up the ladder
destroy the half-formed nest

the bird returns
puzzled but insistent

the exchange continues several days
creating and tearing down

I persist until the bird
vacates to find another space

<114>

I examine the empty transom
should I have been more

supportive and willing
to accommodate a new tenant

let the trees be the landlord
they have more room

<115>

On Walden Pond with Thoreau

Rain today, a fine mist, fog on the pond —
no bird-calls echo through the dense trees;
we push off together, paddle from the shore.

The boat glides on smooth water, slap of oars
lulls us to ponder: why not laze away
a pristine morning? The loon's not here —

We rest, view the scene — on the shore
a tourist parks his SUV by the road, walks to
the water, paces back and forth, confused.

Music from a boom box: rap rhythm
ripples across the pond. Henry feels the beat,
slaps his thighs — old pagan reviving a ritual.

I turn the boat around, offer another view,
swig spring water from a plastic bottle —
Thoreau cups Walden in his hand, drinks.

He smiles — we are invisible, outside time
and space — the image of his bean-rows
twists into the sky, his hut rises into clouds.

Wind ripples the water, a jet marks a long smoky
trail in the sky. A flash of light — he is gone.
I paddle to the shore, wait alone in shadows.

<116>

Meeting Miss Stein

Luxembourg Gardens on spring afternoon:
I meet Gertrude Stein walking her dog
among statues near the carousel.

She pauses, beckons me to join her
forceful stride past the puppet theater,
fountains and early blooming geraniums.

She says — *I'm aware here since some thing
there could always be others perhaps sense what
before I feel we desire that again once before
with no turning both away since here is now*

(My god she speaks like she writes.)

I remark that Paris stimulates me.

She says — *unlike everywhere there can be
no other unlike this one to which knowing
nothing either way forever that is true perhaps
within which much instead remains behind*

Her dog pulls on the leash.

We sit at a café — I study her face.
She resembles Picasso's portrait of her —
he said she would become the painting:
I can't tell her that — she knows.

<117>

She says — *time that is what there can be*
no other than this one here also another
that is present as well like and unlike that links
two who are before different as one by one
pass inside after during and since beyond

She finishes her wine, smiles, rises

floats through flowers —
her dog leads the way.

<118>

ROOM WITH NO VIEW

I take the express train to Florence
as Richard recommended —

> third-class car
> riders with bundles
> food clothing
> bottles in bags
> children sleeping

After four hours arriving weary,
I stumble through the thick burning air
> over winding cobbled streets.

I am at your favorite pensione:
Maria Guduichi's — three flights up —
antiques crowd the room.

Through shutters disturbing slices
of sunlight on the wall,
a spider's web in the dark corner,
shrill voices echo from the courtyard's well.

You stayed here last year.

By early evening the sky fills
with squeaking bats, soaring over red roofs.
I thought they were birds.

I am here not knowing you will never return.

<119>

SCENT OF LILACS

First lilacs bend on late planted bushes,
purple fragrance luring
black and gold bees
who made nests in the garage's moldings.

I tried to exterminate them last summer,
but today one or two hover
near the site.

Is this the longing, melancholy, nostalgia
Johannes Hofer first named: *mal du Suisse*:

Swiss homesickness

mercenaries felt
in 1688 on the plains of France and Italy,
pining for mountain landscapes?

When sent home, many were cured.

I watch the bees circling blooming lilacs
stumble through spring air
confused by a mysterious instinct:
a force driving them
to return home again.

<120>

At the Café Odeon, Zurich, 1915

At Limmatquai 2, neon lights curve
        around the façade — windows glow:

halos illuminate tables, chairs, doorways
        in an Art Nouveau decor.

Crossing borders, time stops for those
        who enter to escape forgotten places.

They leave behind a coat or glove
        but not a way of thinking, writing.

Here's the spirit of James Joyce,
        his thin hand on the stem of a glass

of Fendant — his favorite Swiss wine.
        Don't disturb him.

Exiles cross many borders; each has a tiny box
        easily misplaced,

but remembered when least expected:
        what's in the tiny box?

A tiny ladder reaching down
        an endless bottom to darkness.

<121>

They keep the lid secure: exiles are ghosts,
living in pages of books, folded,

bound for a shelf   inspected at entry,
stamped with no return.

<122>

AT THE CHAT NOIR

Swiss Rudolphe Salis
in Paris, Montmartre, 1881 —
created Chat Noir, a place
for poetry jazz drama —

Theophile Steinlien,
another Swiss, designed
a black cat for the poster
wearing a knowing expression,

who gazed down
on the cabaret,
unmoved by the innovative
music   words   theatrics;

yet, all wanted him there,
reassuring them
of an appreciative audience.

When Rudolphe performed,
scarf draped over his shoulder,
his devoted patrons

drank up life
with gusto
amid the smoke,
applauded his joy of life.

<123>

CARETAKER

He appears at dawn outside Sligo Town
in Drumcliff churchyard, fumbles
with his keys, unlocks the ancient door.

He knows the hymnals are askew —
rights them; the altar is dusty — shines it;
the floor tarnished — removes traces of footsteps.

Purple clouds from the Atlantic bear
gray-blue mist, which wraps around the graveyard's
yew trees, Celtic crosses swept by soft grass;

a granite stone rests alone with the words
Horseman, pass by carved below a revered name;
the caretaker knows the poet was famous —
knows not one poem: yet he senses a closeness.

Spirits ride over Ben Bulben — the green-brown
mountain, shrouded in dark clouds, thrusts its brow
over lush fields where black and white cows linger

near the place where specters thunder in the night:
their hoof-beats resound in the caretaker's reflections
of the mystical — if there are spirits, let them speak;

let them appear. The remains of many rest here:
their grief, loves, hates diminish with days:
the poet's vision remains: his poems, elsewhere.

<124>

MOUNTAIN HIGH

I rise with mist
dawn shifts the earth
tips of trees in the distance
red-winged blackbird flies

dawn shifts the earth
clouds glow deep amber
red-winged blackbird flies
near spirit of the mountain

clouds glow deep amber
ritual incense in the wind
near spirit of the mountain
echoes of timeless chimes

ritual incense in the wind
river speaks to silent stones
echoes of timeless chimes
ancient path to solitude

river speaks to silent stones
tips of trees in the distance
ancient path to solitude
I rise with the mist

<125>

BLOOD-RED MOON

tonight the Sun Earth Moon align
creating a lunar eclipse

Earth's shadow covers the Moon
darkening the sky

the Moon casts a dim reddish hue
from sunlight around Earth's edges

from the Moon the view of both
Earth's sunrise and sunset

blends time together as beginning
and end of the day are one

past and present coalesce
as a series of memories recalled

through shifting shadows
expressed in chosen words

<126>

NOTES ON THE POEMS

Continuum illustrates the importance of how time affects our lives, how each month, day, moment has importance in shaping how we structure our lives and how we deal with the memories from the past as they weave moments into our present. The book divides into three sections: first, the specific description of months, a week, a day; second, the experience of growing up in a small town from ages six to thirteen; third, the adult experiences, which are often surrealistic and set in other countries and times.

"Endless Recall" introduces the main ideas that the following poems develop. The key line "time doesn't stop and the mind/rattles on with endless recall" describes the continuum of unrelated moments or events that "recreate many moments" which will be explored and developed more fully in the poems that follow.

The first series, "January" to "December," evolved from workshop meetings once a month which were affected by the weather. Description is at the beginning of all of them; however, I quickly realized that in each month a particular event emerged, sometimes without my thinking too much about it. As writing about each month continued, I began to realize the poems were not just about passing time but about incidents that shaped a year. The quote in "July" "I perhaps owe it to flowers for having become a painter," is from "Monet: the Artist Speaks," p. 24 CollinsPublishers, San Francisco, 1996.

The second series, "Monday" to "Sunday," began when a neighbor gave me some blueberries. I was reading Chekhov's "Gooseberries" and the coincidence sparked the poem. Slowly I began to realize that in certain days correlations emerged as having similar connections

<127>

to what I was experiencing at a particular moment. They may seem to be about ordinary events, but there are underlying ideas in each day. The quote from "Thursday," "Stones have been known to move," is from Shakespeare's "Macbeth," Act 3, Scene 4, line 122.

The third series, "The Hours," was an experiment to determine if I could write a poem without an "I" speaking or a third person who was the speaker present in the poems. Instead I chose to write from the objective view of an omniscient voice that knows more about what is not happening in the poems than what is described. As the reader moves from "Morning" to "Midnight" the focus is on small things in a kitchen of a person we never meet. All we know is that as the day passes, certain small changes occur — a cup is washed, a napkin is folded, a clock strikes, a dog barks. The continuum is the series of small changes in the room and frequently outside, such as a rain storm. The reader is left to imagine the life of the person who lives in the room by following the slight changes from poem to poem.

"One Second" introduces the second part of "Continuum" expressed as "the past is a country with no borders." The following poems are a journey through several years with very specific incidents and memories arranged in a somewhat chronological order from age nine to fourteen. The poems have a "layered existence" and "memories slide into each other." The events are frequently based on actual experiences often viewed from an adult perspective. I discovered surprises in the days of my childhood that take on extended meaning when shaped into poems.

"In the Shadows" begins with a precocious six-year-old hiding from the outside world as he is unsure of his identity. He aspires to come out of the shadows, gain confidence and to no longer be troubled by gloom. However, some of the details did not happen exactly as in the poem. He speaks as a much older person who is given a voice to recall his distress.

"End of October" is based on actual events that happened to me at age ten when I spent a great deal of time and effort carving a jack-o-lantern only to have it made into a pumpkin pie. Actually

<128>

the old man who died was a neighbor whose presence often confused me. He had been a conductor on the railroad, retired and lived with his daughter who was a devout Catholic. He was not, but his daughter somehow arranged for a Catholic burial. I knelt in front of the coffin as I was told to do, but didn't know what this ritual meant. Those moments still are very vivid in my mind

"The Birdwoman" is based on an actual woman who lived in our town, kept many birds, had few friends and spent a great deal of time walking the streets. Obviously she was somewhat strange and lonely. Our school janitor called her Sacajawea, comparing her to the famous Indian guide for Lewis and Clark. All the kids picked up on the name and were surprised when in history class her name came up as the guide. Some of the details are invented to make the connection between Ava and Sacajawea, but the spirit of the poem integrates them smoothly.

"Poppies" may or may not have happened as narrated in the poem; I remember the poem "In Flanders Field" and the wearing of poppies on November 11; however, I didn't know what they stood for and why everyone wore them; this is a tradition that has lost favor unfortunately. The young boy has a vivid imagination and a poetic mind as the poem reaches a conclusion that only could be explained later in life. "Poppies" first appeared in the *Pittsburgh Post-Gazette* in November 7, 2014.

"Journeys" was inspired by the actual reading of parts of Homer's *Odyssey* in prose. I was fascinated by the section near the end when his dog recognizes him in disguise. But more important was the tree trunk that grew through the floor to make a bed-post. This seemed magical and what I wanted. My father didn't build a tree house, but one exists in the poem which is just as satisfying.

"Baking Day" was part of my mother's continuum. Wash clothes on Monday, iron clothes on Tuesday, bake bread on Wednesday, make noodles or some special dinner on Thursday, create desserts on Friday. We had many relatives who came for Sunday dinner. In the poem my mother sits by the window "lost in thought"; she never talked about all the effort and time she took to prepare these meals and desserts. I was always encouraged to be in the kitchen, to be part of preparing food; it's something that I still enjoy.

<129>

"Open Window, 1942" describes my practicing the piano which I loved to do; I was never forced to spend a certain amount of time going over and over my assigned music. For me, the piano was a way of expressing myself, enjoying the delight of hearing the notes form a continuum of sound. The link between Chopin's heart being taken to Warsaw packed in ice by his sister was part of the uniqueness of his life and death. I didn't know about the death trains in Poland, and when I wrote the poem, the last lines wrote themselves as I felt an approaching storm.

"Almost Twelve" dramatizes the uncertain time in a young man's life when he is caught between childhood which is connected to his climbing trees and having an intimate relationship with them and the moments when he begins to realize and question how he is changing which is described as burning leaves and the ashes of his childhood.

"Arrowhead" is an imaginary response to an actual Indian arrowhead I found when I was working in my father's garden. I still have it and treasure what it represents to me both as a child and an adult.

"Music Lesson" takes place in my piano teacher's house (actually not the place where I had lessons), but I wanted to humanize him with a dog and a garden. He never spoke when I played but wrote down all his comments and gave them to me when I left. My mother baked the best German chocolate cake from my French grandmother's recipe. I loved playing the piano and often had an out-of-body experience.

"Cards" narrates an actual experience, playing Old Maid. There were two sisters who lived on our block who had numerous cats which I loved to play with and pet. There is both cruelty and delight in the way my uncle and father played cards; I often wondered if they were teaching me a lesson or just enjoying making me angry. Either way, I still don't enjoy card games.

"Croquet" represents my neighborhood gang's main pastime in the summer. We played this game for hours in our large level lawn. As an adult looking back, the speaker in the poem realizes that games are a way of preparing for relationships and for life.

<130>

"After the Rain" is based on an actual experience of seeing my grandfather in his coffin; this was the first dead relative I viewed. The estrangement of my father from his father was a very uncomfortable part of our family life. The ritual in the poem is both to free my father from this psychological trauma and to protect me. But how could a dead person hurt me? There are many ways emotional scars are passed from one generation to another. The rain in the poem washes away the unhappy past.

"Tree Talk" is the extension of a noise I heard as a child which links with my close connection to trees. I really believed I could communicate with some special trees.

"Breakfast" dramatizes a recurring incident that shows the distance between me and my father when I was young. The details about getting up and having breakfast alone rather than with him are accurate. We never resolved the issue. My father provided very well for our family, made sure the house was warm in the morning and had a very Swiss breakfast: fried bread topped with melted cheese and an egg. I ate the same combination in a restaurant in Bern, Switzerland years later.

"Flames" traces my fascination with fire, both literal and symbolic. As a child in a small town, burning garbage in a large metal container was standard for all. Burning leaves every fall was a ritual that brought neighbors together. But hell fire was something abstract and found in stories, especially reading about Ulysses in Hell.

"Ritual Rock" like the arrowhead in the garden was found in my yard and takes me back to other eras with the imprint of the leaf on the stone. Here is a visual image from thousands of years ago that is tempting to pick up and remove, but insight makes the young boy somehow realize it is better to leave nature alone.

"Walkers" develops the continuum in this poem through the image of walking. The poem moves between the past and present easily and makes reference to other poems such as "The Birdwoman" and "In the Shadows" and comes full circle as I "stop to measure the moon."

"Chimes" describes accurately my staying with my aunt and the first time sleeping away from home. All the details are clearly

<131>

remembered, particularly her chiming clock which I can still hear. The poem is a contrast to other poems about getting up in the morning and the unspoken motivations of parents. Why did they insist that I stay overnight with my aunt as they knew how she lived and thought about children?

"Words" was a difficult poem to write as words are so important to a poet. I was exposed very early to many types of adult conversations, some agreeable, some hostile. The Irish branch of the family enjoyed disagreements. In contrast, my father's family shared the Swiss characteristic of fewer words and the importance of silence for thinking. When I discovered that my father had limited knowledge of words, I was both frightened and dismayed about how he understood the world we live in. But he had intuition, insight and the benefit of a sharp intelligence that grasped many concepts words could not explain.

"Nightcrawlers" is an imaginary experience with my father who was not a fisherman. The model for the figure in the poem was my much older cousin who came to our yard looking for worms. I felt that writing about him would not give me the opportunity to explore the father and son relationship. However, my distasteful digging for worms is accurate no matter with whom or when.

"The Kingfisher" was written long before "Nightcrawlers" and was inspired by a television documentary about how birds catch fish. There is a dream-like feeling to the experience in the poem which illustrates again the vivid imagination of the young boy.

"Shadows on the Wall" continues the young boy's belief that he is connected to trees or a particular tree. This time the leaves speak to him; he thinks they have a story to tell, but it escapes him and he is "voiceless." Later I wrote this poem to describe the mystery of the scene and the continuing search for meaning in life.

"Fields" describes an actual dream that I had for over ten years: a young boy is in a small French village early in the morning; he doesn't speak but gestures to the distance. Not until I read Carl Jung's autobiography *Memories, Dreams, Reflections*, did I learn that the source of repeated dreams is often linked to an event or a moment in history. Years later as I was doing ancestral research, I learned that one branch of my family came from a small village in

<132>

Alsace-Lorraine in France. When I found the village on the map, I ceased having the dream. Only once, many years later when I was anesthetized for surgery, did the young boy appear again. I do believe that I am that young boy who lived in the 19th century and who looks after me.

"Rain" is a surrealist narrative about a boy who likes books and symbolically dies from reading too much. The rain affects him and others in the poem: the teacher escapes a classroom flood; an elderly woman discovers the boy who is now very small and in her tea cup saucer. She cannot save him from the rain which drowns him because "he cannot swim" or live in the real world; there is a funeral, but is he really dead? This poem first appeared in *The Oakland Review: Alumni Edition*, Carnegie Mellon University, 2011.

"The Sense of Internal Time" is the transition poem to the third section of "Continuum" where several time pieces are described: the Seth Thomas clock in my childhood home, the watch my father always wore and the clock tower in Bern, Switzerland. Accuracy and promptness were important in our house which contribute to my appreciation of time, either external or internal. In this poem I anticipate my writing about other times and places, often they are beyond time or re-imagined specific places.

"Blue Jay" describes an actual meeting with my maternal grandmother who was frozen in time, waiting for her death. She was living with my aunt, the same one in "Chimes" who controlled her and changed her life style. The blue jay mirrors what my grandmother would like to be: free and in nature.

"Strawberries" traces my thoughts about strawberries from age eleven to adulthood. I really did send a love note and chocolate strawberries to an older girl who never acknowledged my gift which hurt me very much. The adult memories of strawberries vary from literature class to an office celebration where we sang "Casey Would Waltz with the Strawberry Blonde" to an older me, sneaking a dessert at night. I find it intriguing that one special fruit keeps turning up in my life.

"Nest" is based on an actual experience of a robin trying to build a nest in our transom which would have made the porch a mess. I had mixed feelings about destroying the nest. She came

<133>

back year after year with persistence, an innate continuum. But finally after three or four years, she gave up; at times practicality overshadows empathy for a homeless creature. I am not fully resigned to my actions.

"Scent of Lilacs" shows the conflict about how to make a decision about nature's creatures. I had to make a choice about having bees exterminated (they were not honey bees) or not. I finally agreed and felt sadness when I saw the results. Strangely, they evoked an historical situation I had read about Swiss mercenaries who had a human instinct to leave the battlefield and return home; they developed an illness called *mal du Suisse*. Every summer I still see one or two bees trying to find the holes they made in the garage, but they soon leave.

"On Walden Pond With Thoreau" imagines a boat ride with the writer — either his ghost or his spirit evoked by my imagination. In contrast, the tourist interrupts the mood. We are "outside time," and he flies away. I am left alone on Walden Pond.

"Room With No View" is a tribute to my friend who died ten years ago. He was very happy that I stayed in the same *pensione* he liked so much. Maria Guduichi was the woman who welcomed me just as she had welcomed my friend. The title is a take-off on Forster's novel, *A Room With a View*. I had a view only of the courtyard well.

"Meeting Miss Stein" is a fantasy about having a conversation with the American writer, Gertrude Stein, who lived in Paris all of her adult life. Her writing is unique and difficult to comprehend as she believed she was creating a new way to express herself. Also, Picasso painted her portrait and left her face blank, saying he would finish it later and she would come to look like the painting. I had a delightful time imagining how Miss Stein would speak, probably not like her writing, but why not?

"At the Café Odeon, Zurich, 1915" draws us into a very famous cafe where exiles from other countries met to share ideas and drink wine. James Joyce and others found refuge in the warmth and congeniality there. The poem imagines Joyce sitting at a table; I often rode the tram at night past the café and had thoughts about what being displaced might be like.

<134>

"At the Chat Noir" describes the cabaret that Rudolphe Salis created for writers, musicians, poets and actors as a place to meet. Salis came from Switzerland to Paris in 1872 and opened Chat Noir in 1885 and was one of the performers. His Swiss friend, Theophile Steinlien, created the famous black-cat posters in the 1880s as well as other works of art. The name "Chat Noir" supposedly came from a stray black cat found on a street lamp when the space was being made into a café. Salis adopted the cat. There is also a possible homage to Edgar Allan Poe's story of the same name.

"Caretaker" is an imaginary man who has the responsibility of caring for the Drumcliff church in the cemetery where the Irish poet, W. B. Yeats, is buried. The details about the mist, the tombstone are all true; the legend of spirits riding horses over the countryside is both fascinating and important in Irish mythology. The poem is about my own experience of being in the churchyard and not mentioning Yeats' name, but giving clues that would identify him.

"Mountain High" is in the form of the pantoum. The "I" in the poem experiences a transformation through nature. This is near the end of "Continuum" as I am moving beyond the earth and say "I rise with the mist."

"Blood-Red Moon" was inspired by a recent eclipse of the blood-red moon. I wondered what the earth would look like if I could be on the moon during the eclipse. With some research, I learned how time on earth is viewed from outer space. The final continuum is expressed in the lines "past and present coalesce" which is what all the poems have been exploring — how everything is connected.

<135>

ABOUT THE AUTHOR

ARTHUR ERBE has been involved with the writing and reading of poetry for most of his career, first as a high school teacher, then as a graduate student at Carnegie Mellon University where he earned a masters and doctorate in literature and writing. At the University of Pittsburgh, he taught a poetry course in the Honors College for 15 years. His interest in writing poetry has been a life-long activity which has been expanded through workshops at Kenyon College, Gettysburg College, the Pittsburgh Center for the Arts, Antioch College and the W. B. Yeats International Summer School in Sligo, Ireland.

For the past ten years he has directed a poetry writing workshop at the Carnegie Library in Oakmont. He has a love of classical music, painting, going to concerts and museums and enjoys playing the piano. For ten years he has been the director of the discussion group of Anton Chekhov's stories that meets monthly. In addition, he is a member of the Swiss-American Society and an officer of the Swiss Nationality Room at the University of Pittsburgh.

He lives in Oakmont, Pennsylvania with his wife, Anne and their two cats, Fellini and Beau Jangles, who are wise and devoted. His wife makes possible an atmosphere of creativity and reflection. Anne, who was an excellent literature and writing teacher is his first and best reader and makes helpful suggestion about specific poems.

Writing the poems gave him a sense of his past and how he cannot forget specific incidents and events that left lasting impressions which are recalled and often expanded by his imagination. Life is a series of moments, some longer than others; however, linking the poems gave him insights not only into his life but how he writes. This process is a continuum that has no end but expansive beginnings.

<136>

ACKNOWLEDGMENTS

I want to thank my poetry teachers: Ann B. Hayes, Carnegie Mellon University; Linda Gregerson, University of Michigan; Maurya Simon, University of California Riverside; John Drury, University of Cincinnati; Ellen Smith, University of Pittsburgh and Alan Dugan, Truro Center for the Arts.

Many thanks to the talented fellow poets of the Allegheny Valley Poets in Oakmont, Pennsylvania. Also thanks to Anne Erbe and Eileen Colianni for their reading of the manuscript and helpful suggestions.

<137>

ABOUT THIS BOOK

The typefaces used in this book are all creations or imitations of designs by Frederic Goudy (1865-1947), one of America's great type designers and fine press printers. Prose sections are set in Goudy Old Style, a font designed by Goudy for American Type-founders in 1915. Loosely based on Italian Renaissance letterforms, the font has distinct features, such as its up-turned hyphen. The italics for this font were inspired by Aldine, a classic Italian font by the pioneering humanist printer Aldus Manutius. The type family was immensely popular, and quickly found its way into phototypesetting and digital font catalogs.

Because Goudy Old Style is not a dense typeface, we chose Goudy Catalogue for the main body type for this book, for higher legibility. This heavier version of Goudy's Old Style typeface was designed by Morris Fuller Benton for American Typefounders in 1919, adding the italic version in 1921.

Poem titles are set in Goudy Catalogue and main titles and section titles are in Goudy Stout.

<138>

www.ingramcontent.com/pod-product-compliance
Lightning Source LLC
LaVergne TN
LVHW091222080426
835509LV00009B/1128